I0082571

2025 Easy Planner
for Activities & Goals

Copyright © 2024 by Paula McDermid / Bainbridge Press

All rights reserved. No part of this book may be reproduced or utilized in any form or by any means, electronic or mechanical, including photocopying, without prior written permission from the author.

ISBN 978-0-9975534-8-2

JANUARY

Holidays & Observances

Jan 1
New Year's Day

Jan 2
Last Day of Chanukah

Jan 6
Epiphany

Jan 7
Orthodox Christmas Day

Jan 10
Asarah B'Tevet

Jan 12
Baptism of Jesus

Jan 14
Orthodox New Year

Jan 20
Martin Luther King Jr. Day

Jan 20
Inauguration Day

Jan 29
Lunar New Year

Sunday	Monday	Tuesday
29	30	31
5	6	7
12	13	14
19	20	21
26	27	28
2	3	4

My monthly calendar

Wednesday	Thursday	Friday	Saturday
1	2	3	4
8	9	10	11
15	16	17	18
22	23	24	25
29	30	31	1
5	6	7	8

My monthly goals

Goals

Goal 1 ....

....

....

Due ....

Goal 2 ....

....

....

Due ....

Goal 3 ....

....

....

Due ....

Goal 4 ....

....

....

Due ....

Tasks for goals

....

....

....

....

....

....

....

....

....

....

....

....

....

....

....

....

....

....

Ideas & Inspiration

♡ ....

♡ ....

♡ ....

♡ ....

My daily plans

Week of ....

Main goals

♡ ....   ♡ ....

....

Monday	Tuesday	Wednesday
....	....	....
....	....	....
....	....	....
....	....	....
....	....	....
....	....	....
....	....	....
....	....	....
....	....	....

Thursday	Friday	Saturday
....	....	....
....	....	....
....	....	....
....	....	....
....	....	**Sunday**
....	....	....
....	....	....
....	....	....
....	....	....

My daily plans

Week of ....

Main goals

♡ .... ♡ ....

....

Monday
....
....
....
....
....
....
....
....
....

Tuesday
....
....
....
....
....
....
....
....
....

Wednesday
....
....
....
....
....
....
....
....
....

Thursday
....
....
....
....
....
....
....
....
....

Friday
....
....
....
....
....
....
....
....
....

Saturday
....
....
....

Sunday
....
....
....
....

JANUARY　My daily plans

Week of ....

Main goals

♡ ....　♡ ....

....　...

Monday
....
....
....
....
....
....
....
....
....

Tuesday
....
....
....
....
....
....
....
....
....

Wednesday
....
....
....
....
....
....
....
....
....

Thursday
....
....
....
....
....
....
....
....
....

Friday
....
....
....
....
....
....

Saturday
....
....
....

Sunday
....
....
....

My daily plans

Week of ....

Main goals

♡ ....   ♡ ....
....

Monday	Tuesday	Wednesday

Thursday	Friday	Saturday
		Sunday

JANUARY   My daily plans

Week of ....

Main goals

♡ ....   ♡ ....
   ....

Monday

Tuesday

Wednesday

Thursday

Friday

Saturday

Sunday

9

FEBRUARY

Holidays & Observances

Feb 2
Candlemas

Feb 10
Asara B'Tevet

Feb 12-13
Tu Bishvat/
Tu B'Shevat

Feb 13-14
Shab-e-Barat

Feb 14
Saint Valentine's
Day

Feb 17
Presidents' Day

Feb 28 or Mar 1
Ramadan begins

Sunday	Monday	Tuesday
26	27	28
2	3	4
9	10	11
16	17	18
23	24	25
2	3	4

My monthly calendar

Wednesday	Thursday	Friday	Saturday
29	30	31	1
5	6	7	8
12	13	14	15
19	20	21	22
26	27	28	1
5	6	7	8

FEBRUARY

My monthly goals

Goals

Goal 1 ....

....

....

Due ....

Goal 2 ....

....

....

Due ....

Goal 3 ....

....

....

Due ....

Goal 4 ....

....

....

Due ....

Tasks for goals

....

....

....

....

....

....

....

....

....

....

....

....

....

....

....

....

....

....

....

....

Ideas & Inspiration

♡ ....

♡ ....

♡ ....

♡ ....

My daily plans

Week of ....

Main goals

♡ ....   ♡ ....

....

Monday

....
....
....
....
....
....
....
....
....

Tuesday

....
....
....
....
....
....
....
....
....

Wednesday

....
....
....
....
....
....
....
....
....

Thursday

....
....
....
....
....
....
....
....
....

Friday

....
....
....
....
....
....
....
....
....

Saturday

....
....
....

Sunday

....
....
....
....

My daily plans

Week of ....

Main goals

♡ ....   ♡ ....

....

Monday	Tuesday	Wednesday
....	....	....
....	....	....
....	....	....
....	....	....
....	....	....
....	....	....
....	....	....
....	....	....
....	....	....

Thursday	Friday	Saturday
....	....	....
....	....	....
....	....	....
....	....	Sunday
....	....	....
....	....	....
....	....	....
....	....	....

My daily plans

Week of ....

Main goals

♡ ....   ♡ ....
....

Monday

....
....
....
....
....
....
....
....
....

Tuesday

....
....
....
....
....
....
....
....
....

Wednesday

....
....
....
....
....
....
....
....
....

Thursday

....
....
....
....
....
....
....
....
....

Friday

....
....
....
....
....
....
....
....
....

Saturday

....
....
....

Sunday

....
....
....
....

My daily plans

Week of ....

Main goals

♡ ....   ♡ ....

....

Monday

....
....
....
....
....
....
....
....
....
....

Tuesday

....
....
....
....
....
....
....
....
....
....

Wednesday

....
....
....
....
....
....
....
....
....
....

Thursday

....
....
....
....
....
....
....
....
....
....

Friday

....
....
....
....
....
....
....
....
....
....

Saturday

....
....
....

Sunday

....
....
....
....

My daily plans

Week of ....

Main goals

♡ ....   ♡ ....
....

Monday
....
....
....
....
....
....
....
....
....

Tuesday
....
....
....
....
....
....
....
....
....

Wednesday
....
....
....
....
....
....
....
....
....

Thursday
....
....
....
....
....
....
....
....
....

Friday
....
....
....
....
....
....
....
....
....

Saturday
....
....
....

Sunday
....
....
....
....

MARCH

Holidays & Observances

Mar 4
Mardi Gras

Mar 5
Ash Wednesday

Mar 9
Daylight Saving Time
starts—U.S.

Mar 13–14
Lent

Mar 13-14
Purim

Mar 17
Saint Patrick's Day

Mar 19
Saint Joseph's Day

Mar 20
March Equinox

Mar 26
Lailat al-Qadr

Mar 27
Feast of the
Annunciation

Mar 29
Ramadan ends

Mar 30
Daylight Saving Time
starts—Europe

Mar 31
Eid al-Fitr

Sunday	Monday	Tuesday
23	24	25
2	3	4
9	10	11
16	17	18
23	24	25
30	31	1

My monthly calendar

Wednesday	Thursday	Friday	Saturday
26	27	28	1
5	6	7	8
12	13	14	15
19	20	21	22
26	27	28	29
2	3	4	5

My monthly goals

Goals	Tasks for goals
Goal 1	....
....	....
....	....
Due	....
	....
Goal 2	....
....	....
....	....
Due	....
	....
Goal 3	....
....	....
....	....
Due	....
	....
Goal 4	....
....	....
....	....
Due	....

Ideas & Inspiration

♡ ....
♡ ....
♡ ....
♡ ....

My daily plans

Week of ....

Main goals

♡ ....   ♡ ....
....

Monday
....
....
....
....
....
....
....
....
....

Tuesday
....
....
....
....
....
....
....
....
....

Wednesday
....
....
....
....
....
....
....
....
....

Thursday
....
....
....
....
....
....
....
....
....

Friday
....
....
....
....
....
....
....
....
....

Saturday
....
....
....
....

Sunday
....
....
....
....

My daily plans

Week of ....

Main goals

♡ .... ♡ ....

....

Monday
....
....
....
....
....
....
....
....
....

Tuesday
....
....
....
....
....
....
....
....
....

Wednesday
....
....
....
....
....
....
....
....
....

Thursday
....
....
....
....
....
....
....
....
....

Friday
....
....
....
....
....
....
....
....
....

Saturday
....
....
....

Sunday
....
....
....

My daily plans

Week of ....

Main goals

♡ ....   ♡ ....
....

Monday	Tuesday	Wednesday
....	....	....
....	....	....
....	....	....
....	....	....
....	....	....
....	....	....
....	....	....
....	....	....

Thursday	Friday	Saturday
....	....	....
....	....	....
....	....	....
....	....	....
....	....	**Sunday**
....	....	....
....	....	....
....	....	....

My daily plans

Week of ....

Main goals

♡ .... ♡ ....

....

Monday	Tuesday	Wednesday

Thursday	Friday	Saturday

Sunday

My daily plans

Week of ....

Main goals

♡ ....   ♡ ....

....

Monday

....
....
....
....
....
....
....
....
....

Tuesday

....
....
....
....
....
....
....
....
....

Wednesday

....
....
....
....
....
....
....
....
....

Thursday

....
....
....
....
....
....
....
....
....

Friday

....
....
....
....
....
....
....
....

Saturday

....
....
....
....

Sunday

....
....
....
....

APRIL

April 1
April Fool's Day

April 5
Eid al-Fitr

April 7
Good Friday

April 12-20
Passover

April 13
Palm Sunday

April 15
Tax Day—U.S.

April 17
Maundy (Holy)
Thursday

April 18
Good Friday

April 19
Holy Saturday

April 20
Easter Sunday

April 22
Earth Day

Sunday	Monday	Tuesday
30	31	1
6	7	8
13	14	15
20	21	22
27	28	29
4	5	6

My monthly calendar

Wednesday	Thursday	Friday	Saturday
2	3	4	5
9	10	11	12
16	17	18	19
23	24	25	26
30	1	2	3
7	8	9	10

My monthly goals

Goals

Goal 1 ....

....

....

Due ....

Goal 2 ....

....

....

Due ....

Goal 3 ....

....

....

Due ....

Goal 4 ....

....

....

Due ....

Tasks for goals

....

....

....

....

....

....

....

....

....

....

....

....

....

....

....

....

Ideas & Inspiration

♡ ....

♡ ....

♡ ....

♡ ....

My daily plans

Week of ....

Main goals

♡ .... ♡ ....
....

Monday
....
....
....
....
....
....
....
....
....

Tuesday
....
....
....
....
....
....
....
....
....

Wednesday
....
....
....
....
....
....
....
....
....

Thursday
....
....
....
....
....
....
....
....
....

Friday
....
....
....
....
....
....
....
....
....

Saturday
....
....
....

Sunday
....
....
....
....

APRIL

My daily plans

Week of ....

Main goals

♡ ....   ♡ ....

....

Monday
....
....
....
....
....
....
....
....
....

Tuesday
....
....
....
....
....
....
....
....
....

Wednesday
....
....
....
....
....
....
....
....
....

Thursday
....
....
....
....
....
....
....
....
....

Friday
....
....
....
....
....
....
....
....
....

Saturday
....
....
....

Sunday
....
....
....
....

My daily plans

Week of ....

Main goals

♡ ....   ♡ ....
   ....

Monday
....
....
....
....
....
....
....
....
....

Tuesday
....
....
....
....
....
....
....
....
....

Wednesday
....
....
....
....
....
....
....
....
....

Thursday
....
....
....
....
....
....
....
....

Friday
....
....
....
....
....
....
....
....

Saturday
....
....
....
....

Sunday
....
....
....
....

My daily plans

Week of ....

Main goals

♡ ....   ♡ ....

....

Monday

....
....
....
....
....
....
....
....
....

Tuesday

....
....
....
....
....
....
....
....
....

Wednesday

....
....
....
....
....
....
....
....
....

Thursday

....
....
....
....
....
....
....
....
....

Friday

....
....
....
....
....
....
....
....
....

Saturday

....
....
....

Sunday

....
....
....
....

My daily plans

Week of ....

Main goals

♡ ....   ♡ ....
....

Monday
....
....
....
....
....
....
....
....
....

Tuesday
....
....
....
....
....
....
....
....
....

Wednesday
....
....
....
....
....
....
....
....
....

Thursday
....
....
....
....
....
....
....
....
....

Friday
....
....
....
....
....
....
....
....
....

Saturday
....
....
....
....

Sunday
....
....
....
....

MAY

Sunday	Monday	Tuesday
27	28	29
4	5	6
11	12	13
18	19	20
25	26	27
1	2	3

My monthly calendar

Wednesday	Thursday	Friday	Saturday
30	1	2	3
7	8	9	10
14	15	16	17
21	22	23	24
28	29	30	31
4	5	6	7

My monthly goals

Goals

Goal 1 ....

....

....

Due ....

Goal 2 ....

....

....

Due ....

Goal 3 ....

....

....

Due ....

Goal 4 ....

....

....

Due ....

Tasks for goals

....

....

....

....

....

....

....

....

....

....

....

....

....

....

....

....

Ideas & Inspiration

♡ ....

♡ ....

♡ ....

♡ ....

My daily plans

Week of ....

Main goals

♡ ....   ♡ ....

....

Monday

Tuesday

Wednesday

Thursday

Friday

Saturday

Sunday

My daily plans

Week of ....

Main goals

♡ ....   ♡ ....

....

Monday

....
....
....
....
....
....
....
....
....

Tuesday

....
....
....
....
....
....
....
....
....

Wednesday

....
....
....
....
....
....
....
....
....

Thursday

....
....
....
....
....
....
....
....
....

Friday

....
....
....
....
....
....
....
....
....

Saturday

....
....
....

Sunday

....
....
....
....

MAY

My daily plans

Week of ....

Main goals

♡ ....   ♡ ....
....

Monday
....
....
....
....
....
....
....
....
....

Tuesday
....
....
....
....
....
....
....
....
....

Wednesday
....
....
....
....
....
....
....
....
....

Thursday
....
....
....
....
....
....
....
....
....

Friday
....
....
....
....
....
....
....
....
....

Saturday
....
....
....

Sunday
....
....
....

My daily plans

Week of ....

Main goals

♡ ....   ♡ ....

....

Monday
....
....
....
....
....
....
....
....

Tuesday
....
....
....
....
....
....
....
....

Wednesday
....
....
....
....
....
....
....
....

Thursday
....
....
....
....
....
....
....
....

Friday
....
....
....
....
....
....
....
....

Saturday
....
....
....

Sunday
....
....
....
....

My daily plans

Week of ....

Main goals

♡ ....   ♡ ....
....

Monday
....
....
....
....
....
....
....
....
....

Tuesday
....
....
....
....
....
....
....
....
....

Wednesday
....
....
....
....
....
....
....
....
....

Thursday
....
....
....
....
....
....
....
....
....

Friday
....
....
....
....
....
....
....
....
....

Saturday
....
....
....

Sunday
....
....
....
....
....

JUNE

Holidays & Observances

June 1-3
Shavuot

June 5-9
Hajj

June 7-10
Eid-al-Adha

June 8
Pentecost

June 9
Whit Monday

June 15
Trinity Sunday

June 15
Father's Day

June 19
Feast of Corpus
Christi

June 19-20
Juneteenth

June 20
June Solstice

Jun 26
Hirja

June 27
Muharram

June 29
Feasts of Saints
Peter and Paul

Sunday	Monday	Tuesday
1	2	3
8	9	10
15	16	17
22	23	24
29	30	1
6	7	8

My monthly calendar

Wednesday	Thursday	Friday	Saturday
4	5	6	7
11	12	13	14
18	19	20	21
25	26	27	28
2	3	4	5
9	10	11	12

My monthly goals

Goals	Tasks for goals
Goal 1	....
....	....
....	....
Due	....
	....
Goal 2	....
....	....
....	....
Due	....
	....
Goal 3	....
....	....
....	....
Due	....
	....
Goal 4	....
....	....
....	....
Due	....

Ideas & Inspiration

♡ ....
♡ ....
♡ ....
♡ ....

JUNE

My daily plans

Week of ....

Main goals

♡ ....   ♡ ....
....

Monday

....
....
....
....
....
....
....
....
....

Tuesday

....
....
....
....
....
....
....
....
....

Wednesday

....
....
....
....
....
....
....
....
....

Thursday

....
....
....
....
....
....
....
....
....

Friday

....
....
....
....
....
....
....
....
....

Saturday

....
....
....
....

Sunday

....
....
....
....
....

My daily plans

Week of ....

Main goals

♡ ....   ♡ ....
....

Monday
....
....
....
....
....
....
....
....
....

Tuesday
....
....
....
....
....
....
....
....
....

Wednesday
....
....
....
....
....
....
....
....
....

Thursday
....
....
....
....
....
....
....
....
....

Friday
....
....
....
....
....
....
....

Saturday
....
....
....

Sunday
....
....
....
....

My daily plans

Week of ....

Main goals

♡ ....   ♡ ....
  ....

Monday
....
....
....
....
....
....
....
....
....
....

Tuesday
....
....
....
....
....
....
....
....
....
....

Wednesday
....
....
....
....
....
....
....
....
....
....

Thursday
....
....
....
....
....
....
....
....
....

Friday
....
....
....
....
....
....
....
....
....

Saturday
....
....
....
....

Sunday
....
....
....
....

My daily plans

Week of ....

Main goals

♡ .... ♡ ....

....

Monday

Tuesday

Wednesday

Thursday

Friday

Saturday

Sunday

My daily plans

Week of ....

Main goals

♡ ....   ♡ ....
....

Monday

Tuesday

Wednesday

Thursday

Friday

Saturday

Sunday

JULY

July 1
Canada Day

July 4
Independence
Day—U.S.

July 4-5
Ashura

July 15
Saint Vladimir Day

July 13-Aug 3
Bein ha-Metzarim

July 14
Bastille Day

July 18
Nelson Mandela Day

July 25
Feast Day of Saint
James the Great

Sunday	Monday	Tuesday
29	30	1
6	7	8
13	14	15
20	21	22
27	28	29
3	4	5

My monthly calendar

Wednesday	Thursday	Friday	Saturday
2	3	4	5
9	10	11	12
16	17	18	19
23	24	25	26
30	31	1	2
6	7	8	9

JULY

My monthly goals

Goals

Goal 1 ....

....

....

Due ....

Goal 2 ....

....

....

Due ....

Goal 3 ....

....

....

Due ....

Goal 4 ....

....

....

Due ....

Tasks for goals

....

....

....

....

....

....

....

....

....

....

....

....

....

....

....

....

Ideas & Inspiration

♡ ....

♡ ....

♡ ....

♡ ....

My daily plans

Week of ....

Main goals

♡ ....   ♡ ....
....

Monday
....
....
....
....
....
....
....
....

Tuesday
....
....
....
....
....
....
....
....

Wednesday
....
....
....
....
....
....
....
....

Thursday
....
....
....
....
....
....
....
....

Friday
....
....
....
....
....
....
....
....

Saturday
....
....
....
....

Sunday
....
....
....
....

My daily plans

Week of ....

Main goals

♡ ....   ♡ ....
....

Monday	Tuesday	Wednesday

Thursday	Friday	Saturday
		Sunday

JULY

My daily plans

Week of ....

Main goals

♡ ....   ♡ ....

....

Monday
....
....
....
....
....
....
....
....
....

Tuesday
....
....
....
....
....
....
....
....
....

Wednesday
....
....
....
....
....
....
....
....
....

Thursday
....
....
....
....
....
....
....
....
....

Friday
....
....
....
....
....
....
....
....
....

Saturday
....
....
....
....

Sunday
....
....
....
....

My daily plans

Week of ....

Main goals

♡ ....   ♡ ....

....

Monday

....
....
....
....
....
....
....
....
....

Tuesday

....
....
....
....
....
....
....
....
....

Wednesday

....
....
....
....
....
....
....
....
....

Thursday

....
....
....
....
....
....
....
....
....

Friday

....
....
....
....
....
....
....
....
....

Saturday

....
....
....

Sunday

....
....
....
....

My daily plans

Week of ....

Main goals

♡ .... ♡ ....

....

Monday

....
....
....
....
....
....
....
....
....

Tuesday

....
....
....
....
....
....
....
....
....

Wednesday

....
....
....
....
....
....
....
....
....

Thursday

....
....
....
....
....
....
....
....
....

Friday

....
....
....
....
....
....
....
....
....

Saturday

....
....
....

Sunday

....
....
....
....

AUGUST

Holidays & Observances

Aug 2-3
Tish'a B'Av

Aug 8-9
Tu B'Av

Aug 15
Assumption
of Mary

Aug 24
Feast of Saint
Bartholomew

Sunday	Monday	Tuesday
27	28	29
3	4	5
10	11	12
17	18	19
24	25	26
31	1	2

My monthly calendar

Wednesday	Thursday	Friday	Saturday
30	31	1	2
6	7	8	9
13	14	15	16
20	21	22	23
27	28	29	30
3	4	5	6

My monthly goals

Goals

Goal 1 ....

....

....

Due ....

Goal 2 ....

....

....

Due ....

Goal 3 ....

....

....

Due ....

Goal 4 ....

....

....

Due ....

Tasks for goals

....

....

....

....

....

....

....

....

....

....

....

....

....

....

....

....

Ideas & Inspiration

♡ ....

♡ ....

♡ ....

♡ ....

AUGUST

My daily plans

Week of ....

Main goals

♡ ....   ♡ ....

....

Monday

....
....
....
....
....
....
....
....
....

Tuesday

....
....
....
....
....
....
....
....
....

Wednesday

....
....
....
....
....
....
....
....
....

Thursday

....
....
....
....
....
....
....
....

Friday

....
....
....
....
....
....
....
....

Saturday

....
....
....

Sunday

....
....
....
....

My daily plans

Week of ....

Main goals

♡ ....   ♡ ....

....

Monday
....
....
....
....
....
....
....
....
....

Tuesday
....
....
....
....
....
....
....
....
....

Wednesday
....
....
....
....
....
....
....
....
....

Thursday
....
....
....
....
....
....
....
....
....

Friday
....
....
....
....
....
....
....
....
....

Saturday
....
....
....

Sunday
....
....
....
....

My daily plans

Week of ....

Main goals

♡ .... ♡ ....

....

Monday
....
....
....
....
....
....
....
....
....

Tuesday
....
....
....
....
....
....
....
....
....

Wednesday
....
....
....
....
....
....
....
....
....

Thursday
....
....
....
....
....
....
....
....
....

Friday
....
....
....
....
....
....
....
....

Saturday
....
....
....

Sunday
....
....
....
....

My daily plans

Week of ....

Main goals

♡ .... ♡ ....
  ....

Monday	Tuesday	Wednesday
....	....	....
....	....	....
....	....	....
....	....	....
....	....	....
....	....	....
....	....	....
....	....	....

Thursday	Friday	Saturday
....	....	....
....	....	....
....	....	....
....	....	....
....	....	**Sunday**
....	....	....
....	....	....
....	....	....
....	....	....

My daily plans

Week of ....

Main goals

♡ ....   ♡ ....

....

Monday

Tuesday

Wednesday

Thursday

Friday

Saturday

Sunday

SEPTEMBER

Holidays & Observances

Sept 1
Labor Day

Sept 4-5
Mawlid Un Nabi

Sept 11
Patriot Day

Sept 13
Selichot

Sept 14
Holy Cross Day

Sept 21
Saint Matthew Day

Sept 22
September Equinox

Sept 22-24
Rosh Hashanah

Sunday	Monday	Tuesday
31	1	2
7	8	9
14	15	16
21	22	23
28	29	30
5	6	7

My monthly calendar

Wednesday	Thursday	Friday	Saturday
3	4	5	6
10	11	12	13
17	18	19	20
24	25	26	27
1	2	3	4
8	9	10	11

My monthly goals

Goals

Goal 1 ....

....

....

Due ....

Goal 2 ....

....

....

Due ....

Goal 3 ....

....

....

Due ....

Goal 4 ....

....

....

Due ....

Tasks for goals

....

....

....

....

....

....

....

....

....

....

....

....

....

....

....

....

....

....

....

....

Ideas & Inspiration

♡ ....

♡ ....

♡ ....

♡ ....

My daily plans

Week of ....

Main goals

♡ ....   ♡ ....
....

Monday

....
....
....
....
....
....
....
....

Tuesday

....
....
....
....
....
....
....
....

Wednesday

....
....
....
....
....
....
....
....

Thursday

....
....
....
....
....
....
....
....

Friday

....
....
....
....
....
....
....
....

Saturday

....
....
....

Sunday

....
....
....
....

My daily plans

Week of ....

Main goals

♡ .... ♡ ....

....

Monday

....
....
....
....
....
....
....
....

Tuesday

....
....
....
....
....
....
....
....

Wednesday

....
....
....
....
....
....
....
....

Thursday

....
....
....
....
....
....
....
....

Friday

....
....
....
....
....
....
....
....

Saturday

....
....
....

Sunday

....
....
....
....

My daily plans

Week of ....

Main goals

♡ ....   ♡ ....

....

Monday

....
....
....
....
....
....
....
....
....

Tuesday

....
....
....
....
....
....
....
....
....

Wednesday

....
....
....
....
....
....
....
....
....

Thursday

....
....
....
....
....
....
....
....
....

Friday

....
....
....
....
....
....
....
....
....

Saturday

....
....
....
....

Sunday

....
....
....
....

My daily plans

Week of ....

Main goals

♡ .... ♡ ....

....

Monday
....
....
....
....
....
....
....
....
....

Tuesday
....
....
....
....
....
....
....
....
....

Wednesday
....
....
....
....
....
....
....
....
....

Thursday
....
....
....
....
....
....
....
....
....

Friday
....
....
....
....
....
....
....
....
....

Saturday
....
....
....

Sunday
....
....
....

My daily plans

Week of ....

Main goals

♡ ....   ♡ ....
....

Monday	Tuesday	Wednesday
....	....	....
....	....	....
....	....	....
....	....	....
....	....	....
....	....	....
....	....	....
....	....	....
....	....	....

Thursday	Friday	Saturday
....	....	....
....	....	....
....	....	....
....	....	....
....	....	Sunday
....	....	....
....	....	....
....	....	....
....	....	....

OCTOBER

Sunday	Monday	Tuesday
28	29	30
5	6	7
12	13	14
19	20	21
26	27	28
2	3	4

My monthly calendar

Wednesday	Thursday	Friday	Saturday
1	2	3	4
8	9	10	11
15	16	17	18
22	23	24	25
29	30	31	1
5	6	7	8

My monthly goals

Goals   Tasks for goals

Goal 1 ....
....
....
Due ....
                                              ....
Goal 2 ....
....
....
Due ....
                                              ....
Goal 3 ....
....
....
Due ....
                                              ....
Goal 4 ....
....
....
Due ....

Ideas & Inspiration
♡ ....
♡ ....
♡ ....
♡ ....

My daily plans

Week of ....

Main goals

♡ ....   ♡ ....
    ....

Monday	Tuesday	Wednesday
....	....	....
....	....	....
....	....	....
....	....	....
....	....	....
....	....	....
....	....	....
....	....	....

Thursday	Friday	Saturday
....	....	....
....	....	....
....	....	....
....	....	**Sunday**
....	....	....
....	....	....
....	....	....
....	....	....

My daily plans

Week of ....

Main goals

♡ .... ♡ ....

....

Monday

....
....
....
....
....
....
....
....
....

Tuesday

....
....
....
....
....
....
....
....
....

Wednesday

....
....
....
....
....
....
....
....
....

Thursday

....
....
....
....
....
....
....
....
....

Friday

....
....
....
....
....
....
....
....
....

Saturday

....
....
....

Sunday

....
....
....

My daily plans

Week of ....

Main goals

♡ ....   ♡ ....

....

Monday

....
....
....
....
....
....
....
....
....

Tuesday

....
....
....
....
....
....
....
....
....

Wednesday

....
....
....
....
....
....
....
....
....

Thursday

....
....
....
....
....
....
....
....
....

Friday

....
....
....
....
....
....
....
....
....

Saturday

....
....
....

Sunday

....
....
....
....

My daily plans

Week of ....

Main goals

♡ ....   ♡ ....
....

Monday
....
....
....
....
....
....
....
....
....
....

Tuesday
....
....
....
....
....
....
....
....
....
....

Wednesday
....
....
....
....
....
....
....
....
....
....

Thursday
....
....
....
....
....
....
....
....
....
....

Friday
....
....
....
....
....
....
....
....
....
....

Saturday
....
....
....

Sunday
....
....
....

My daily plans

Week of ....

Main goals

♡ ....   ♡ ....
....

Monday
....
....
....
....
....
....
....
....
....

Tuesday
....
....
....
....
....
....
....
....
....

Wednesday
....
....
....
....
....
....
....
....
....

Thursday
....
....
....
....
....
....
....
....
....

Friday
....
....
....
....
....
....
....
....
....

Saturday
....
....
....

Sunday
....
....
....
....

NOVEMBER

Sunday	Monday	Tuesday
26	27	28
2	3	4
9	10	11
16	17	18
23	24	25
30	1	2

My monthly calendar

Wednesday	Thursday	Friday	Saturday
29	30	31	1
5	6	7	8
12	13	14	15
19	20	21	22
26	27	28	29
3	4	5	6

My monthly goals

Goals

Goal 1 ....

....

....

Due ....

Goal 2 ....

....

....

Due ....

Goal 3 ....

....

....

Due ....

Goal 4 ....

....

....

Due ....

Tasks for goals

....

....

....

....

....

....

....

....

....

....

....

....

....

....

....

....

Ideas & Inspiration

♡ ....

♡ ....

♡ ....

♡ ....

My daily plans

Week of ....

Main goals

♡ ....   ♡ ....
....

Monday
....
....
....
....
....
....
....
....
....

Tuesday
....
....
....
....
....
....
....
....
....

Wednesday
....
....
....
....
....
....
....
....
....

Thursday
....
....
....
....
....
....
....
....
....

Friday
....
....
....
....
....
....
....
....
....

Saturday
....
....
....

Sunday
....
....
....
....

My daily plans

Week of ....

Main goals

♡ ....   ♡ ....

....

Monday
....
....
....
....
....
....
....
....
....
....

Tuesday
....
....
....
....
....
....
....
....
....
....

Wednesday
....
....
....
....
....
....
....
....
....
....

Thursday
....
....
....
....
....
....
....
....
....
....

Friday
....
....
....
....
....
....
....
....
....
....

Saturday
....
....
....

Sunday
....
....
....
....

My daily plans

Week of ....

Main goals

♡ .... 　 ♡ ....
　.. 　 　..

Monday

Tuesday

Wednesday

Thursday

Friday

Saturday

Sunday

My daily plans

Week of ....

Main goals

♡ ....   ♡ ....

....

Monday

....
....
....
....
....
....
....
....
....

Tuesday

....
....
....
....
....
....
....
....
....

Wednesday

....
....
....
....
....
....
....
....
....

Thursday

....
....
....
....
....
....
....
....
....

Friday

....
....
....
....
....
....
....
....
....

Saturday

....
....
....

Sunday

....
....
....

NOVEMBER   My daily plans

Week of ....

Main goals
♡ ....   ♡ ....
  ....

Monday
....
....
....
....
....
....
....
....
....

Tuesday
....
....
....
....
....
....
....
....
....

Wednesday
....
....
....
....
....
....
....
....
....

Thursday
....
....
....
....
....
....
....
....
....

Friday
....
....
....
....
....
....
....
....
....

Saturday
....
....
....

Sunday
....
....
....
....

DECEMBER

Holidays &
Observances

Dec 6
Saint Nicholas Day

Dec 7
Second Sunday
of Advent

Dec 8
Immaculate
Conception

Dec 7
Third Sunday
of Advent

Dec 14-22
Chanukah/Hanukkah

Dec 21
December Solstice

Dec 21
Fourth Sunday
of Advent

Dec 24
Christmas Eve

Dec 25
Christmas Day

Dec 26-Jan 1
Kwanzaa

Dec 27
Saint John Day

Dec 30
Asara B'Tevet

Dec 31
New Year's Eve

Sunday	Monday	Tuesday
30	1	2
7	8	9
14	15	16
21	22	23
28	29	30
4	5	6

My monthly calendar

Wednesday	Thursday	Friday	Saturday
3	4	5	6
10	11	12	13
17	18	19	20
24	25	26	27
31	1	2	3
7	8	9	10

DECEMBER My monthly goals

Goals

Goal 1 ....

....

....

Due ....

Goal 2 ....

....

....

Due ....

Goal 3 ....

....

....

Due ....

Goal 4 ....

....

....

Due ....

Tasks for goals

....

....

....

....

....

....

....

....

....

....

....

....

....

....

....

....

....

....

Ideas & Inspiration

♡ ....

♡ ....

♡ ....

♡ ....

My daily plans

Week of ....

Main goals

♡ ....   ♡ ....
  ....

Monday
....
....
....
....
....
....
....
....
....

Tuesday
....
....
....
....
....
....
....
....
....

Wednesday
....
....
....
....
....
....
....
....
....

Thursday
....
....
....
....
....
....
....
....
....

Friday
....
....
....
....
....
....
....
....
....

Saturday
....
....
....
....

Sunday
....
....
....
....

My daily plans

Week of ....

Main goals

♡ ....   ♡ ....
....

Monday
....
....
....
....
....
....
....
....
....

Tuesday
....
....
....
....
....
....
....
....
....

Wednesday
....
....
....
....
....
....
....
....
....

Thursday
....
....
....
....
....
....
....
....

Friday
....
....
....
....
....
....
....
....

Saturday
....
....
....

Sunday
....
....
....

My daily plans

Week of ....

Main goals

♡ ....   ♡ ....

....

Monday
....
....
....
....
....
....
....
....

Tuesday
....
....
....
....
....
....
....
....

Wednesday
....
....
....
....
....
....
....
....

Thursday
....
....
....
....
....
....
....
....

Friday
....
....
....
....
....
....
....
....

Saturday
....
....
....
....

Sunday
....
....
....
....

My daily plans

Week of ....

Main goals

♡ ....   ♡ ....

....

Monday
....
....
....
....
....
....
....
....
....

Tuesday
....
....
....
....
....
....
....
....
....

Wednesday
....
....
....
....
....
....
....
....
....

Thursday
....
....
....
....
....
....
....
....

Friday
....
....
....
....
....
....
....
....

Saturday
....
....
....

Sunday
....
....
....

My daily plans

Week of ....

Main goals

♡ .... ♡ ....

....

Monday	Tuesday	Wednesday
....	....	....
....	....	....
....	....	....
....	....	....
....	....	....
....	....	....
....	....	....
....	....	....
....	....	....

Thursday	Friday	Saturday
....	....	....
....	....	....
....	....	....
....	....	....
....	....	Sunday
....	....	....
....	....	....
....	....	....
....	....	....

Books by this Author

More information at www.paula-mcdermid.com

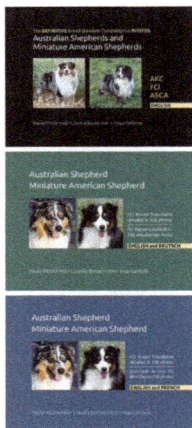

For breeders and judges of Australian Shepherds and Miniature American Shepherds

The Definitive Breed Standard Comparison in Photos for Australian Shepherds and Miniature American Shepherds. AKC, FCI, ASCA. English

Australian Shepherd, Miniature American Shepherd: FCI Breed Standards detailed in 238 photos.
English and Deutsch

Australian Shepherd, Miniature American Shepherd: FCI Breed Standards detailed in 238 photos.
English and French

For breeders of Australian Shepherds

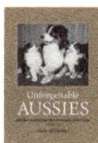

Genealogy and history of 15 influential Australian Shepherd sires and dams who were descendants of the Flintridge foundation dogs.
> *Unforgettable Aussies. Australian Shepherd Dogs Who Left Pawprints on Our Hearts.*
> Volume I: 1970 to 1994.

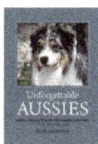

Genealogy and history of 12 influential Australian Shepherd sires and dams who were descendants of the Flintridge foundation dogs.
> *Unforgettable Aussies. Australian Shepherd Dogs Who Left Pawprints on Our Hearts.*
> Volume II: 1995 to 2000.

www.ingramcontent.com/pod-product-compliance
Lightning Source LLC
Chambersburg PA
CBHW051248020426
42333CB00025B/3110